Greatest Ever

Fish

The All Time Top 20 Greatest Recipes

Greatest Ever

Fish

The All Time Top 20 Greatest Recipes

p

This is a Parragon Book
First published in 2002

Parragon
Queen Street House
4 Queen Street
Bath BA1 1HE, UK

Copyright © Parragon 2002

All rights reserved. No part of this publication may be reproduced,
stored in a retrieval system or transmitted, in any form or by any means,
electronic, mechanical, photocopying, recording or otherwise, without
the prior permission of the copyright holder.

ISBN: 0-75256-855-8

Printed in China

NOTE

This book uses metric and imperial measurements. Follow the same
units of measurement throughout; do not mix metric and imperial.
All spoon measurements are level: teaspoons are assumed to be 5 ml,
and tablespoons are assumed to be 15 ml. Unless otherwise stated,
milk is assumed to be full fat, eggs and individual vegetables such as
potatoes are medium, and pepper is freshly ground black pepper.

The times given for each recipe are an approximate guide only because the
preparation times may differ according to the techniques used by different
people and the cooking times may vary as a result of the type of oven used.
The preparation times include the marinating times, where appropriate.

Recipes using raw or very lightly cooked eggs should be
avoided by infants, the elderly, pregnant women, convalescents,
and anyone suffering from an illness.

C O N T E N T S

6   INTRODUCTION

12   PASTA & HERRING SALAD

13   SALADE NIÇOISE

14   SMOKED MACKEREL PÂTÉ

15   GARLIC PRAWN KEBABS

16   THAI-STYLE FISH CAKES

17   CALAMARI

18   CULLEN SKINK

19   GIANT GARLIC PRAWNS

20   HERB-ROASTED COD

21   SEAFOOD RISOTTO WITH OREGANO

22   MOULES MARINIÈRES

23   PASTA PUTTANESCA

24   SEAFOOD LASAGNE

25   SMOKED FISH PIE

26   KEDGEREE

27   COD & CHIPS

28   JAMBALAYA

29   SKATE WITH BLACK BUTTER

30   DOVER SOLE À LA MEUNIÈRE

31   FIVE-SPICE SALMON

32   INDEX

INTRODUCTION

There are many different types of fish to suit different tastes, including white fish such as cod and haddock, cartilaginous fish such as skate, and oily fish such as mackerel, salmon and tuna. This huge range of textures and flavours guarantees that fish is never dull, and suits many types of accompaniments, from sharp sauces and spicy butters to rice and fresh vegetables. It is quick to prepare and cook, with little waste, which makes it good value for money.

The argument for increasing the amount of fish and shellfish we eat makes excellent sense. Seafood is generally high in protein and low in calories. Oily fish are rich in healthy unsaturated fats.

Whether you are shopping for fish in a supermarket or at your local fishmonger, to get the freshest fish look out for clear, sparkling, moist eyes, bright red or pink gills, flesh which springs back when you press it with your thumb, and a fresh smell of the sea, with no hint of 'fishiness'. Oysters, mussels and clams should have tightly closed shells. Tap any that are gaping slightly – if they don't close at once, leave well alone. Cooked shellfish should be sweet smelling, with no hint of ammonia.

prawn

lobster

Above: Lobsters can be bought alive – their dark blue shells turn pink when cooked. Prawns can be bought fresh or frozen, in or out of their shells.

H A N D L I N G   F I S H

Storage

As you can rarely be sure how long ago a fish was caught, you are better off cooking it on the day you buy it.

If that is not practicable, but you are likely to use it within a couple of days, put the fish in a plastic container and sprinkle some ice over the top. Then cover it with a sheet of clingfilm and store it in the coldest part of the refrigerator for no more than two days. Otherwise, it is best to freeze the fish as soon as you can.

Firm fish, such as turbot, Dover sole and monkfish, freeze much better than softer ones, such as plaice or lemon sole. Always thaw frozen fish slowly and thoroughly before cooking.

salmon fillet

Below: Whole fish are easy to prepare with a little practice. Or you can ask your fishmonger.

rainbow trout

sardines

Preparation

The amount of descaling, gutting, filleting and skinning your fish needs depends largely on where you buy it. Many supermarkets sell ready-trimmed fresh fish on trays covered with clingfilm from a chiller cabinet. Most have a wet-fish counter with an expert fishmonger on hand who will fillet the whole fish of your choice at no extra charge.

It is fairly straightforward, however, to buy a whole fish and prepare it yourself. With a little practice and a sharp knife, you will soon get the hang of filleting.

Generally, you don't need many special tools or pieces of equipment for preparing and cooking fish.

juicer

lemons

orange

fish slice

cook's knife

lemon zester

E Q U I P M E N T

Utensils

The most useful utensils for fish cookery are:

★ A large easy-to-clean plastic chopping board set aside specifically for raw fish. Like meat, raw and cooked fish should always be prepared separately. For safety's sake, sit the chopping board on a tea-towel or a folded newspaper to steady it while you are pulling off the fish skin.

★ A sharp, thin-bladed, flexible filleting knife for taking the fish off the bone and skinning it.

★ A small pair of eyebrow tweezers, which will be invaluable for plucking out small bones.

★ A fish slice for lifting pieces of fish into and out of the pan without flaking or falling apart.

Cookware

If you are planning to cook a whole fish as a centre-piece for a buffet party, a fish kettle would be a wise investment. This is a large oblong pan with a lifting tray on which to sit the fish and a lid to cover it. If you only need to use it very rarely, you may be able to hire one from a local cookery shop or even a friendly fishmonger. Otherwise, you could share the cost with a few friends and take turns in using it.

A wok or large, heavy-based frying pan is a boon for frying and stir-frying fish. You can also use a wok for steaming, by sitting the fish on a perforated platform over boiling water. A bamboo steamer basket or a pizza tray both work well.

For deep-frying fish in batter or breadcrumbs you need a large, deep pan with a wire-mesh basket to fit inside. Use the basket for holding chips or breaded fish but not for battered fillets, as the raw batter wraps around the strands of wire as it cooks and gets stuck.

mussels

small sharp knife

frying pan

Above: The versatility of fish means that basic cookery equipment is often all that you need to try your hand at a few fish recipes.

COOKING METHODS

griddle

Certain cooking methods are better suited to different fish. On the whole, moist methods, such as poaching, steaming and stewing, produce more succulent results than grilling, barbecuing or baking. However, if the fish is cooked quickly at a high enough temperature, the drying out effect can be minimized.

sardines

Poaching

Immerse the fish in the recommended poaching liquid, which may be fish stock, milk, beer or cider. Bring the liquid to the boil. As soon as it is boiling, remove the pan from the heat and leave the fish to finish cooking in the residual heat. This helps to avoid overcooking and is ideal if you want to serve the fish cold.

Steaming

As a gentle cooking technique, steaming is good for preserving the taste and texture of delicately flavoured fish and shellfish. Again, you can use a flavoured liquid, which will impart some of its flavour to the fish as it cooks.

roasting trays

large saucepan
with lid

Stewing

Steaky fish, either whole or cut into smaller pieces, are best for cooking in a liquid with vegetables as a stew.

Grilling

This is one of the quickest and easiest ways of cooking fish, either whole or as steaks and fillets. Make sure that the grill is on its highest setting and very hot before you start cooking the fish. Position the fish as close to the heat source as possible without charring it.

tarragon

Barbecuing

If barbecuing outdoors, brush the fish with butter, oil or marinade before and during cooking to keep it moist.

Baking and roasting

This covers all methods of cooking fish in the oven, including open roasting, casseroling or *en papillote* (in foil or greaseproof paper parcels).

Shallow- and pan-frying

This is a quick method of cooking fish and shellfish. Heat a shallow layer of oil or butter and oil in a frying pan, add the fish and cook on one side for 2 minutes before carefully turning it over to cook on the other side for a further 1–2 minutes, until just tender and lightly browned. A heavy-based, non-stick frying pan makes life a lot easier when undertaking this type of cooking.

potatoes

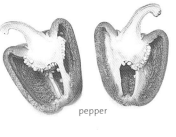

pepper

Above: A variety of vegetables can be used to make stock for poaching.

leeks

Deep-frying

The fish is covered in batter or breadcrumbs to protect it from direct contact with the very hot oil. Large pieces of fish in batter are best cooked at 180°C/350°F which allows the fish time to cook without burning the batter. Smaller pieces of fish, like thin strips (goujons) in breadcrumbs, are best cooked at a slightly higher temperature of 190°C/375°F. Drain deep-fried items well on kitchen paper to keep them crisp.

steamer

PASTA & HERRING SALAD

> Serves 4 > Preparation time: 30 minutes > Cooking time: 15 minutes

INGREDIENTS

250 g/9 oz dried pasta shells

5 tbsp olive oil

400 g/14 oz rollmop herrings in brine

6 boiled potatoes

2 large tart apples

2 baby frisée lettuces

2 baby beetroot

4 hard-boiled eggs

6 pickled onions

6 pickled gherkins

2 tbsp capers

3 tbsp of tarragon vinegar

salt and pepper

METHOD

1 Bring a large saucepan of lightly salted water to the boil. Add the pasta and 1 tablespoon of the olive oil, and cook until tender but firm to the bite. Drain, and refresh in cold water.

2 Cut the herrings, potatoes, apples, frisée lettuces and beetroot into small pieces. Put all of these ingredients into a large salad bowl.

3 Drain the pasta thoroughly and add to the salad bowl. Toss lightly to combine the pasta with the herring mixture. Season.

4 Carefully shell the hard-boiled eggs, then slice. Garnish the salad with the slices of egg, pickled onions, pickled gherkins and capers, sprinkle with the remaining olive oil and the tarragon vinegar, season to taste and serve.

SALADE NIÇOISE

›Serves 4   ›Preparation time: 20 minutes   ›Cooking time: 25 minutes

INGREDIENTS

3 large eggs

250 g/9 oz French beans, topped and tailed

250 g/9 oz small waxy potatoes, such as
Charlottes, scrubbed and halved

1 large, sun-ripened tomato, cut into eighths

1 large tuna steak, about 350 g/12 oz and
2 cm/³/₄ inch thick, seared

55 g/2 oz Provençal-style olives or plain
black olives

50 g/1³/₄ oz canned anchovy fillets in oil,
drained

1 tbsp chopped fresh flat-leaved parsley

GARLIC VINAIGRETTE

100 ml/3¹/₂ fl oz extra-virgin olive oil

3 tbsp red or white wine vinegar

¹/₂ tsp sugar

¹/₂ tsp Dijon mustard

2 garlic cloves, crushed

salt and pepper

METHOD

1 To make the vinaigrette, put all the
ingredients in a screw-top jar and shake until
blended. Season with salt and pepper to taste.
Set aside.

2 Boil the eggs for 12 minutes. Drain them and
refresh them under cold running water to stop
them cooking further.

3 Put the beans and potatoes into separate
pans of boiling water. Blanch the beans for
3 minutes, then drain and immediately transfer
to a large bowl. Shake the dressing and pour
it over the beans. Cook the potatoes until
tender, then drain and add to the beans and
dressing while still hot. Leave to cool.

4 Add the tomato, break the seared tuna into
large chunks and gently toss with the other
ingredients. Shell the eggs and then cut them
into quarters.

5 Mound the tuna and vegetables on a large
serving platter and surround with the eggs.
Scatter with olives and add a lattice of
anchovies. Cover and chill.

6 About 15 minutes before serving, remove the
salad from the refrigerator and sprinkle with
the chopped parsley.

13

SMOKED MACKEREL PÂTÉ

> Serves 4 → Preparation time: 30 minutes plus overnight chilling
> Cooking time: 5–10 minutes

INGREDIENTS

200 g/7 oz smoked mackerel fillet

1 small hot green chilli, deseeded and chopped

1 garlic clove, chopped

3 tbsp fresh coriander leaves

150 ml/5 fl oz soured cream

1 small red onion, chopped

2 tbsp lime juice

salt and pepper

4 slices white bread, crusts removed

METHOD

1 Skin and flake the mackerel, removing any small bones. Put the flesh in the bowl of a food processor along with the chilli, garlic, coriander and soured cream. Blend until smooth.

2 Transfer the mixture to a bowl and mix in the onion and lime juice. Season to taste. The pâté will seem very soft at this stage but will firm up in the refrigerator. Refrigerate for several hours or overnight if possible.

3 The pâté is served with melba toast. To make it, place the trimmed bread slices under a preheated medium grill and toast lightly on one side. Split each piece in half horizontally, then cut these across diagonally to form 4 triangles per slice.

4 Put the melba toast triangles, untoasted side up, under the grill and toast them until they are golden and curled at the edges. Serve the toast warm or cold with the pâté.

GARLIC PRAWN KEBABS

> Serves 4 > Preparation time: 50 minutes > Cooking time: 12 minutes

INGREDIENTS

350 g/12 oz raw prawns, peeled and deveined

2 tbsp chopped fresh parsley

4 tbsp lemon juice

2 tbsp olive oil

5 tbsp butter

2 garlic cloves, chopped

salt and pepper

METHOD

1 Place the prawns in a shallow, non-metallic dish with the parsley and lemon juice and season with salt and pepper to taste. Cover and set aside to marinate in the herb mixture for at least 30 minutes.

2 Heat the oil and butter in a small pan with the garlic until the butter melts. Stir to mix.

3 Remove the prawns from the marinade with a draining spoon and add them to the pan containing the garlic butter. Stir until well coated, then thread the prawns on to skewers.

4 Barbecue the kebabs over hot coals for 5–10 minutes, turning the skewers occasionally, until the prawns turn pink and are cooked through. Brush the prawns with the remaining garlic butter during the cooking time. Alternatively, cook under a preheated grill, turning and brushing frequently with the garlic butter.

5 Transfer the prawn kebabs to warmed serving plates. Drizzle over any of the remaining garlic butter and serve.

THAI-STYLE FISH CAKES

>Serves 4 >Preparation time: 10 minutes >Cooking time: 20 minutes

INGREDIENTS

450 g/1 lb cod fillets, skinned

2 tbsp fish sauce

2 red Thai chillies, deseeded and finely chopped

2 garlic cloves, crushed

10 lime leaves, finely chopped

2 tbsp chopped fresh coriander

1 large egg

25 g/1 oz plain flour

100 g/3½ oz fine green beans, finely sliced

groundnut oil, for frying

METHOD

1 Using a sharp knife, roughly cut the cod fillets into bite-sized pieces.

2 Place the cod pieces in a food processor together with the fish sauce, chillies, garlic, lime leaves, coriander, egg and plain flour. Process until finely chopped and turn out into a large mixing bowl.

3 Add the green beans to the bowl and mix.

4 Divide the mixture into small balls. Flatten the balls between the palms of your hands to form rounds.

5 Heat a little oil in a preheated wok. Fry the fish cakes on both sides until brown and crispy on the outside.

6 Transfer the fish cakes to serving plates and serve hot.

CALAMARI

>Serves 4   >Preparation time: 25 minutes   >Cooking time: 10 minutes

INGREDIENTS

115 g/4 oz plain flour

1 tsp salt

2 eggs

175 ml/6 fl oz soda water

500 g/1 lb 2 oz whole squid

vegetable oil, for deep-frying

TO GARNISH

lemon wedges

fresh parsley sprigs

METHOD

1 Sift the flour into a bowl with the salt. Add the eggs and half the soda water and whisk together until smooth. Gradually whisk in the remaining soda water until the batter is smooth. Set aside.

2 To prepare the squid, hold each one firmly and grasp the tentacles just inside the body. Pull firmly to remove the innards. Find the transparent quill and remove. Grasp the wings on the outside of the body and pull to remove the outer skin. Trim the tentacles just below the beak and reserve.

3 Wash the prepared bodies and tentacles under running water. Slice the bodies across into 1-cm/$\frac{1}{2}$-inch rings. Drain on kitchen paper.

4 Meanwhile, fill a deep saucepan about a third full with vegetable oil and heat to 190°C/375°F/Gas Mark 5, or until a cube of bread browns in 30 seconds.

5 Dip the squid rings and tentacles into the batter, a few at a time, and drop into the hot oil. Fry for 1–2 minutes until crisp and golden. Drain on kitchen paper. Cook all the squid this way. Serve while hot, garnished with lemon slices and parsley.

CULLEN SKINK

>Serves 4   >Preparation time: 20 minutes   >Cooking time: 40 minutes

INGREDIENTS

225 g/8 oz undyed smoked haddock fillet

2 tbsp butter

1 onion, finely chopped

600 ml/1 pint milk

350 g/12 oz potatoes, diced

350 g/12 oz cod, boned, skinned and cubed

150 ml/5 fl oz double cream

2 tbsp chopped fresh parsley

lemon juice, to taste

salt and pepper

TO GARNISH

fresh parsley sprigs

lemon slices

METHOD

1 Put the haddock in a large frying pan and cover with boiling water. Leave for 10 minutes. Drain, reserving 300 ml/10 fl oz of the soaking water. Flake the fish and remove all the bones.

2 Heat the butter in a large saucepan and add the onion. Cook gently for 10 minutes until softened. Add the milk and bring to a gentle simmer before adding the potatoes. Cook for 10 minutes.

3 Add the reserved haddock flakes and cod. Simmer for a further 10 minutes until the cod is tender.

4 Remove about one-third of the fish and potatoes, put in a food processor and blend until smooth. Alternatively, push the mixture through a sieve into a bowl. Return to the soup with the cream, parsley and seasoning. Taste and add a little lemon juice, if desired. Add a little of the reserved soaking water if the soup seems too thick. Reheat gently, and serve garnished with parsley and lemon slices.

18

GIANT GARLIC PRAWNS

>Serves 4   >Preparation time: 5 minutes   >Cooking time: 5–7 minutes

INGREDIENTS

125 ml/4 fl oz olive oil

4 garlic cloves, finely chopped

2 hot red chillies, deseeded and
finely chopped

450 g/1 lb cooked king prawns

2 tbsp chopped fresh flat-leaved parsley

salt and pepper

crusty bread, to serve

lemon wedges, to garnish

METHOD

1 Heat the oil in a large frying pan over a low
heat. Add the garlic and chillies and cook for
1–2 minutes until softened but not coloured.

2 Add the prawns and stir-fry for 2–3 minutes
until heated through and coated in the oil
and garlic mixture. Remove from the heat.

3 Add the parsley and stir well to mix. Season
to taste.

4 Divide the prawns and garlic oil between
warmed serving dishes and serve with lots of
crusty bread. Garnish with lemon wedges.

HERB-ROASTED COD

›Serves 4   ›Preparation time: 10–15 minutes   ›Cooking time: 25–30 minutes

INGREDIENTS

2 tbsp butter

50 g/1¾ oz fresh wholemeal breadcrumbs

25 g/1 oz chopped walnuts

grated rind and juice of 2 lemons

2 sprigs fresh rosemary, stalks removed

2 tbsp chopped fresh parsley

4 cod fillets, about 150 g/5½ oz each

1 garlic clove, crushed

1 small red chilli, diced

3 tbsp walnut oil

salad leaves, to serve

METHOD

1 Melt the butter in a large frying pan, then remove from the heat.

2 Add the breadcrumbs, walnuts, the rind and juice of 1 lemon, half of the rosemary and half of the parsley and mix.

3 Press the breadcrumb mixture over the top of the cod fillets. Place the fillets in a shallow, foil-lined roasting tin.

4 Bake in a preheated oven at 200°C/400°F/Gas Mark 6 for 25–30 minutes.

5 Mix together the garlic, chilli, and the remaining lemon rind and juice, rosemary and parsley in a bowl. Beat in the walnut oil and mix to combine. Drizzle the dressing over the cod steaks as soon as they are cooked.

6 Transfer to serving plates and serve with salad leaves.

SEAFOOD RISOTTO WITH OREGANO

›Serves 4   ›Preparation time: 5 minutes   ›Cooking time: 25 minutes

INGREDIENTS

1.2 litres/2 pints hot fish or chicken stock

350 g/12 oz arborio rice, washed

4 tbsp butter

2 garlic cloves, chopped

250 g/9 oz mixed seafood, preferably raw, such as prawns, squid, mussels, clams and shrimps

2 tbsp chopped fresh oregano, plus extra for garnishing

50 g/1¾ oz pecorino or Parmesan cheese, grated

METHOD

1 In a large pan, bring the stock to the boil. Add the rice and cook for about 12 minutes, stirring, until the rice is tender, or according to the instructions on the packet. Drain thoroughly, reserving any liquid.

2 Heat the butter in a large frying pan and add the garlic, stirring.

3 Add the mixed seafood to the pan. If the seafood is raw, cook for 5 minutes; if it is already cooked, reduce the time to about 2–3 minutes.

4 Stir the oregano into the seafood mixture in the frying pan.

5 Add the cooked rice to the pan and cook for 2–3 minutes, stirring, or until hot. Add the reserved stock if the mixture gets too sticky.

6 Add the pecorino or Parmesan cheese and mix well.

7 Transfer the seafood risotto to warm dishes and serve.

MOULES MARINIÈRES

❯Serves 4   ❯Preparation time: 40 minutes   ❯Cooking time: 20 minutes

INGREDIENTS

2 kg/4 lb 8 oz live mussels

4 tbsp olive oil

4–6 large garlic cloves, halved

2 x 400 g/14 oz cans chopped tomatoes

300 ml/10 fl oz dry white wine

2 tbsp finely chopped fresh flat-leaved parsley, plus extra for garnishing

1 tbsp finely chopped fresh oregano

salt and pepper

French bread, to serve

METHOD

1 Leave the mussels to soak in a bowl of lightly salted water for 30 minutes. Rinse them under cold running water and lightly scrub to remove any sand from the shells. Using a small, sharp knife, remove the 'beards' from the shells.

2 Discard any broken or open mussels that do not shut when tapped firmly with the back of a knife. This indicates that they are dead and could cause food poisoning if eaten. Rinse the mussels again, then set aside in a colander.

3 Heat the olive oil in a large saucepan or stockpot over a medium-high heat. Add the garlic and fry, stirring, for about 3 minutes to flavour the oil. Using a slotted spoon, remove the garlic from the pan.

4 Add the tomatoes and their juice, the wine, parsley and oregano and bring to the boil, stirring. Lower the heat, cover and simmer for 5 minutes to allow the flavours to blend.

5 Add the mussels, cover and simmer for 5–8 minutes, shaking the pan regularly, until they open. Using a slotted spoon, transfer them to serving bowls, discarding any that are not open.

6 Season the sauce with salt and pepper to taste. Ladle the sauce over the mussels, sprinkle with extra parsley and serve with plenty of French bread to mop up the juices.

PASTA PUTTANESCA

>Serves 4 >Preparation time: 5 minutes >Cooking time: 30 minutes

INGREDIENTS

3 tbsp extra-virgin olive oil

1 large red onion, finely chopped

4 anchovy fillets, drained

pinch of chilli flakes

2 garlic cloves, finely chopped

400 g/14 oz canned chopped tomatoes

2 tbsp tomato purée

225 g/8 oz dried spaghetti

25 g/1 oz pitted black olives, roughly chopped

25 g/1 oz pitted green olives, roughly chopped

1 tbsp capers, drained and rinsed

4 sun-dried tomatoes, roughly chopped

salt and pepper

METHOD

1 Heat the oil in a saucepan and add the onion, anchovies and chilli flakes. Cook for 10 minutes until softened and starting to brown. Add the garlic and cook for 30 seconds.

2 Add the tomatoes and tomato purée to the pan and bring to the boil, then simmer gently for 10 minutes.

3 Meanwhile, cook the spaghetti in plenty of salted boiling water, according to the packet instructions, until it is tender but still firm to the bite.

4 Add the olives, capers and sun-dried tomatoes to the sauce. Simmer for a further 2–3 minutes. Season to taste.

5 Drain the pasta thoroughly and pour in the anchovy sauce. Toss together so the pasta is well coated with sauce and serve.

SEAFOOD LASAGNE

>Serves 4 >Preparation time: 10 minutes >Cooking time: 45 minutes

INGREDIENTS

450 g/1 lb finnan haddock, filleted, skin removed and flesh flaked

115 g/4 oz prawns

115 g/4 oz sole fillet, skin removed and flesh sliced

juice of 1 lemon

450g/1 lb pre-cooked lasagne

55 g/2 oz freshly grated Parmesan cheese

pepper

SAUCE

4 tbsp butter

3 leeks, very thinly sliced

55 g/2 oz plain flour

about 600 ml/1 pint milk

2 tbsp clear honey

200g/7 oz grated mozzarella cheese

METHOD

1 Put the haddock fillet, prawns and sole fillet into a large bowl and season with pepper and lemon juice to taste. Cover the bowl and set it aside while you make the sauce.

2 Melt the butter in a large saucepan. Add the leeks and cook, stirring occasionally, for 8 minutes. Add the flour and cook, stirring constantly, for 1 minute. Gradually stir in enough milk to make a thick, creamy sauce.

3 Blend in the honey and mozzarella cheese and continue cooking for a further 3 minutes. Remove the pan from the heat and mix in the fish and prawns.

4 Make alternate layers of fish sauce and lasagne in an ovenproof dish, finishing with a layer of fish sauce on top. Generously sprinkle over the grated Parmesan cheese and bake in a preheated oven, 180°C/350°F/Gas Mark 4, for 30 minutes. Serve hot.

SMOKED FISH PIE

›Serves 4   ›Preparation time: 10 minutes   ›Cooking time: 1½ hours

INGREDIENTS

2 tbsp olive oil

1 onion, finely chopped

1 leek, thinly sliced

1 carrot, diced

1 celery stick, diced

115 g/4 oz button mushrooms, halved

grated rind of 1 lemon

700 g/1 lb 9 oz skinless white fish, half smoked cod or haddock, half unsmoked haddock, hake or monkfish, cubed

225 g/8 oz peeled cooked prawns

2 tbsp chopped fresh parsley

1 tbsp chopped fresh dill

salt and pepper

SAUCE

4 tbsp butter

35 g/1¼ oz plain flour

1 tsp mustard powder

600 ml/1 pint milk

85 g/3 oz Gruyère cheese, grated

TOPPING

675 g/1½ lb potatoes, cooked in ther skins

4 tbsp butter, melted

4 tbsp grated Gruyère cheese

METHOD

1 For the sauce, melt the butter in a large pan and add the flour and mustard powder. Stir until smooth. Cook over a low heat for 2 minutes without colouring. Gradually whisk in the milk until smooth. Simmer gently for 2 minutes, then stir in the cheese until melted. Remove the pan from the heat and put a piece of clingfilm over the surface of the sauce to prevent a skin from forming. Set aside.

2 Heat the olive oil in a clean pan and add the onion. Fry over a low heat, stirring occasionally, for 5 minutes. Add the leek, carrot, celery and mushrooms and cook for 10 minutes, stirring occasionally. Stir in the grated lemon rind.

3 Add the vegetables to the sauce with the fish, prawns, parsley and dill. Season, and transfer to a greased 1.7-litre/3-pint casserole.

4 For the topping, peel the cooked potatoes, grate them and mix with the melted butter. Cover the fish and vegetable mixture with the potato and sprinkle with the grated cheese.

5 Cover loosely with foil. Bake in a preheated oven, 200°C/400°F/Gas Mark 6, for 30 minutes. Remove the foil and bake for 30 minutes until the topping is golden. Serve hot.

KEDGEREE

›Serves 4 ›Preparation time: 5 minutes ›Cooking time: 45 minutes

INGREDIENTS

450 g/1 lb undyed smoked haddock fillet

2 tbsp olive oil

1 large onion, chopped

2 garlic cloves, finely chopped

½ tsp ground turmeric

½ tsp ground cumin

1 tsp ground coriander

175 g/6 oz basmati rice

4 medium eggs

2 tbsp butter

1 tbsp chopped fresh parsley

TO SERVE

lemon wedges

mango chutney

METHOD

1 Pour boiling water over the haddock fillet and leave for 10 minutes. Lift the fish from the cooking water, reserving the liquid. Discard the skin and bones and flake the flesh. Set aside.

2 Heat the oil in a large saucepan and add the onion. Cook for 10 minutes over a medium heat until starting to brown. Add the garlic and cook for a further 30 seconds. Add the turmeric, cumin and coriander and stir-fry for 30 seconds until the spices smell fragrant. Add the rice and stir well.

3 Measure 350 ml/12 fl oz of the haddock cooking water and add this to the saucepan. Stir well and bring to the boil. Cover and cook over a very low heat for 12–15 minutes until the rice is tender and the stock is absorbed.

4 Meanwhile, bring a small saucepan of water to the boil and add the eggs. When the water has returned to the boil, cook the eggs for 8 minutes. Immediately drain the eggs and refresh them under cold running water to stop them cooking further. Set them aside.

5 Mix the reserved pieces of haddock and the butter and fresh parsley into the rice. Turn the rice on to a large serving dish. Shell and quarter the hard-boiled eggs and arrange them on top of the rice. Serve the kedgeree with lemon wedges and mango chutney.

COD & CHIPS

>Serves 4   >Preparation time: 1½ hours   >Cooking time: 40 minutes

INGREDIENTS

900 g/2 lb old potatoes

vegetable oil, for deep-frying

4 x 175 g/6 oz thick cod fillets

salt and pepper

lemon wedges, to serve

fresh parsley sprigs, to garnish

BATTER

15 g/½ oz fresh yeast

300 ml/10 fl oz beer

225 g/8 oz plain flour

2 tsp salt

MAYONNAISE

1 egg yolk

1 tsp wholegrain mustard

1 tbsp lemon juice

200 ml/7 fl oz extra-virgin olive oil

salt and pepper

METHOD

1 For the batter, cream the yeast with a little beer until smooth. Gradually stir in the rest of the beer. Sift the flour and salt into a bowl, make a well in the centre and add the yeast mixture. Whisk to a smooth batter. Cover and leave at room temperature for 1 hour.

2 For the mayonnaise, put the egg yolk, mustard, lemon juice and seasoning into a food processor. Blend for 30 seconds until frothy. Begin adding the olive oil, drop by drop, until the mixture begins to thicken. Continue adding the oil in a slow, steady stream until it has been incorporated. Season to taste. Refrigerate until needed.

3 Cut the potatoes into chips about 1 cm/½ inch thick. Heat a large pan half filled with vegetable oil until a cube of bread browns in 1 minute. Cook the chips, in 2 batches, for about 5 minutes, until cooked through but not browned. Drain on kitchen paper and set aside.

4 Increase the temperature of the oil until a cube of bread browns in 45 seconds. Season the fish, dip in batter and fry, 2 pieces at a time, for 7–8 minutes until golden and cooked through. Drain on kitchen paper. Keep warm.

5 Increase the temperature of the oil until a cube of bread browns in 30 seconds. Fry the chips again, in 2 batches, for 2–3 minutes until crisp and golden. Drain on kitchen paper and sprinkle with salt.

6 Serve the fish and chips with mayonnaise and lemon wedges, garnished with parsley.

JAMBALAYA

> Serves 4   > Preparation time: 5 minutes   > Cooking time: 30 minutes

INGREDIENTS

2 tbsp vegetable oil

2 onions, roughly chopped

1 green pepper, deseeded and roughly chopped

2 celery sticks, roughly chopped

3 garlic cloves, finely chopped

2 tsp paprika

300 g/10½ oz skinless, boneless chicken breasts, chopped

100 g/3½ oz kabanos sausages, chopped

3 tomatoes, skinned and chopped

450 g/1 lb long-grain rice

850 ml/1½ pints hot chicken or fish stock

1 tsp dried oregano

2 fresh bay leaves

12 large prawn tails

4 spring onions, finely chopped

2 tbsp chopped fresh parsley

salt and pepper

salad, to serve

METHOD

1 Heat the vegetable oil in a large frying pan and add the onions, pepper, celery and garlic. Cook for 8–10 minutes until all the vegetables have softened. Add the paprika and cook for a further 30 seconds. Add the chicken and sausages and cook for 8–10 minutes until lightly browned. Add the tomatoes and cook for 2–3 minutes until collapsed.

2 Add the rice to the pan and stir well. Pour in the hot stock, oregano and bay leaves and stir well. Cover and simmer for 10 minutes over a very low heat.

3 Add the prawn tails and stir well. Cover again and cook for a 6–8 minutes until the rice is tender and the prawns are cooked through.

4 Stir in the spring onions and parsley, and season to taste. Serve with a salad.

SKATE WITH BLACK BUTTER

>Serves 4   >Preparation time: 5 minutes   >Cooking time: 1¼ hours

INGREDIENTS

900 g/2 lb skate wings, in 4 pieces

175 g/6 oz butter

3 tbsp red wine vinegar

15 g/½ oz capers, drained

1 tbsp chopped fresh parsley

salt and pepper

COURT-BOUILLON

850 ml/1½ pints cold water

850 ml/1½ pints dry white wine

3 tbsp white wine vinegar

2 large carrots, roughly chopped

1 onion, roughly chopped

2 celery sticks, roughly chopped

2 leeks, roughly chopped

2 garlic cloves, roughly chopped

2 fresh bay leaves

4 sprigs fresh parsley

4 sprigs fresh thyme

6 black peppercorns

1 tsp salt

TO SERVE

new potatoes

green vegetables

METHOD

1 For the court-bouillon, put all of the ingredients into a large saucepan and bring slowly to the boil. Cover and simmer gently for 30 minutes. Strain the liquid through a fine sieve into a clean pan. Bring to the boil again and simmer fast, uncovered, for 15–20 minutes, until reduced to 600 ml/1 pint.

2 Place the skate wing in a wide shallow pan and pour the court-bouillon over them. Bring to the boil and simmer gently for 15 minutes, or a little longer depending on the thickness of the skate. Drain the fish and set aside, keeping it warm.

3 Meanwhile, melt the butter in a frying pan. Cook over a medium heat until the butter becomes a dark brown and smells nutty.

4 Add the vinegar, capers and parsley and allow to simmer for 1 minute. Season to taste with salt and pepper. Pour over the fish. Serve immediately with boiled new potatoes and a seasonal fresh green vegetable.

DOVER SOLE À LA MEUNIÈRE

> Serves 4 > Preparation time: 10 minutes > Cooking time: 15 minutes

INGREDIENTS

35 g/1¼ oz plain flour

1 tsp salt

4 Dover soles, about 400 g/14 oz each, cleaned and skinned

150 g/5½ oz butter

3 tbsp lemon juice

1 tbsp chopped fresh parsley

¼ of a preserved lemon, finely chopped (optional)

salt and pepper

lemon slices, to garnish

METHOD

1 Mix the flour with the salt and place on a large plate or tray. Drop the fish into the flour, one at a time, and shake well to remove any excess. Melt 40 g/1½ oz (3 tablespoons) of the butter in a small saucepan and use to brush the fish liberally all over.

2 Place the fish under a preheated hot grill and cook for 5 minutes each side.

3 Meanwhile, melt the remaining butter in a pan. Pour cold water into a bowl large enough to take the base of the pan. Keep nearby.

4 Heat the butter until it turns a golden brown and begins to smell nutty. Remove immediately from the heat and immerse the base of the pan in the cold water, to stop further cooking.

5 Put the fish on to individual serving plates, drizzle with the lemon juice and sprinkle with the parsley and preserved lemon, if using. Pour over the browned butter and serve, garnished with lemon slices.

FIVE-SPICE SALMON

>Serves 4   >Preparation time: 15 minutes   >Cooking time:15 minutes

INGREDIENTS

4 salmon fillets, 125 g/4¹/₂ oz each, skinned

2 tsp Chinese five-spice powder

1 large leek

1 large carrot

115 g/4 oz mangetouts

2.5-cm/1-inch piece fresh root ginger

2 tbsp ginger wine

2 tbsp light soy sauce

1 tbsp vegetable oil

salt and pepper

TO GARNISH

shredded leek

shredded fresh root ginger

shredded carrot

METHOD

1 Wash the salmon and pat dry on kitchen paper. Rub the five-spice powder into both sides of the fish and season with salt and pepper. Set aside until required.

2 Trim the leek, slice it down the centre and rinse under cold water to remove any dirt. Finely shred the leek. Peel the carrot and cut it into very thin strips. Top and tail the mangetouts and cut them into shreds. Peel the ginger and slice thinly into strips.

3 Place all of the vegetables into a large bowl and toss in the ginger wine and 1 tablespoon of the soy sauce.

4 Preheat the grill to medium. Place the salmon fillets on the rack and brush with the remaining soy sauce. Cook for 2–3 minutes on each side until cooked through.

5 While the salmon is cooking, heat the oil in a non-stick wok or large frying pan and stir-fry the vegetables for 5 minutes until just tender, taking care not to overcook them. Transfer to serving plates. Drain the salmon on kitchen paper and serve on the beds of vegetables. Garnish with shredded leek, ginger and carrot.

INDEX

B

baking 11

barbecuing 11

C

calamari 17

cod & chips 27

cooking methods 10–11

cookware 9

Cullen skink 18

D

deep-frying 9, 11

Dover sole à la
    meunière 30

F

filleting 7, 8

fish kettles 9

five-spice salmon 31

freezing 7

frying 9, 11

E

equipment 10–11

G

garlic prawn kebabs 15

giant garlic prawns 19

grilling 10

H

herb-roasted cod 20

J

jambalaya 28

K

kedgeree 26

M

moules marinières 22

P

pasta & herring salad 12

pasta puttanesca 23

poaching 10

preparation 7

protein 6

R

roasting 11

S

salade Niçoise 13

seafood lasagne 24

seafood risotto 21

skate with black butter 29

smoked fish pie 25

smoked mackerel pâté 14

steaming 9, 10

stewing 10

stir-frying 9

storage 7

T

Thai-style fish cakes 16

thawing 7

U

unsaturated fats 6

utensils 8

W

woks 9